A LITTLE
OF SUSS

GW00721829

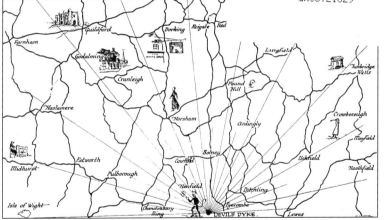

Helen Poole

S.B. Publications

By the same author
Lewes Priory, the Site and its History. (Lewes Priory Trust 2000)
Lewes Past (Phillimore 2000)
Old Hitchin: Portrait of an English Market Town (with Alan Fleck 1976)
Here for the Beer (Watford Museum 1984)
Watford and the Civil War (Watford Borough Council 1989)

First published in 2001 by S. B. Publications

©Helen Poole

ISBN 1 85770 243 3

Designed and typeset by CGB, Lewes
Printed by Tansleys The Printers 19 Broad Street, Seaford, East Sussex BN25 1LS
Telephone: (01323) 891019

CONTENTS

INTRODUCTION

What makes Sussex special? Everyone will have ideas on this, whether they are Sussex born and bred, or an incomer like me. The locals proclaim that 'Sussex won't be druv' and this spirit of independence has meant that the county has suffered less than many others in the pursuit of modernity. This book attempts to give a feel of Sussex in its many guises, to share our delight in the county we love. Happily we walk in the footsteps of Belloc and Kipling, the Bloomsbury group and many more, so the choice is almost endless.

I have lived in Sussex for fifteen years and worked for the Sussex Archaeological Society for ten, so I know part of the county very well and other parts not at all. This book is dedicated to those who enjoy Sussex as much as I do and have shared their enthusiasms with me.

Helen Poole
Haywards Heath
September 2001

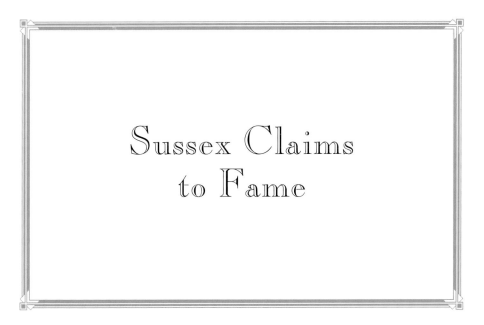

Sussex Claims
to Fame

The highest point in the county is Black Down, 919 feet above sea level. It stands on the northern greensand ridge to the north west of Sussex, near the Surrey border.

Boxgrove Man is currently the oldest known European, dating back half a million years. His age is based on surviving shin bones and the presence of a particular type of vole near the findspot. He pushes the Kent claimant, Swanscombe Man (actually a woman) into second place.

Dr Gideon Mantell of Lewes was one of the first men in England to realise that the bones that he found were from dinosaurs, particularly the iguanodon. He and his wife uncovered the fossilised fragments of this 25ft dinosaur near

Cuckfield in the sandstone of Tilgate Forest and he announced this discovery to the Royal Society in 1825.

One of the greatest hoaxes in prehistory was the Piltdown Man, 'found' in a gravel pit at Barkham Vineyard in 1912 and championed by Charles Dawson, an Uckfield solicitor and amateur antiquary. The skull was claimed as that of a Lower Pleistocene man, some 150,000 years old, but tests in London and Oxford in 1953 showed that the cranium belonged to an Upper Pleistocene man, a mere 50,000 years old, attached to a jaw and canine tooth of a modern ape, carefully faked to simulate great age. This gave rise to the ingenious crossword clue, 'Skullduggery in Sussex'.

Master Huggett and his man John
They did make the first cannon.

The first cast iron cannon was made at Buxted in 1543, by Peter Baude, a French founder, and Ralph Hogge or Huggett, perhaps inspired by the

Rector of Buxted, William Levett. From then on, for 200 years the Weald enjoyed an almost total monopoly of iron-gun casting, a vital part of England's defence. Thomas Fuller found it incredible that so many great guns were made in Sussex and wondered whether they had done more harm than printing.

John Norden in his *Surveyor's Dialogue* of 1607 said that there were in Sussex nearly 140 hammers and furnaces for iron, each of which consumed every 24 hours from two to four loads of charcoal. But there was, he thought, some doubt whether the clearance was altogether hurtful, since 'people bred among woods are naturally more stubborn and uncivil than in the champain countries.'

For centuries the oak was so common in Sussex that it was known as the 'Sussex weed'. At least ten per cent of the county is still wooded, although the gale of 16 October 1987 wiped out nearly three million oaks. Sussex is the second most wooded county in England.

Ditchling claims to have the world's oldest flower show. The Ditchling Fruit Society was founded c. 1824 'for the purpose of encouraging the culture of useful fruits and plants in the garden and neighbourhood, but more particularly as a stimulus to the working classes of society who have hitherto sadly neglected this profitable and amusing employ.' A history of the village in 1901 reported:

At the Annual Show ... surely it may be said with safety that such splendid specimens as are there exhibited are not to be met with at any other place in the kingdom, and so fine are they that they have been known to sell at sevenpence each. This is the famed Ditchling gooseberry. The Ditchling gardeners are to be complimented on the perfection to which they have attained in rearing this luscious fruit.

☆ ☆ ☆

In 1902 Frances Viscountess Wolseley set up the Glynde School for Lady Gardeners at Ragged Lands. Although women had been able to train as gardeners since 1891, this college was specifically for ladies and was run on military lines, as befitted the daughter of the Boer War Field Marshal. The College was aimed at educated women, the daughters of professional men, but for the maidservant or secondary-school girl it would seem that farm and not garden life holds out far more suitable prospects.' In 1908 when an agricultural worker would have earned £1 a week, her fees were £10 per year. The College closed during the First World War.

William Huskisson MP was the first man to be killed by a train when he fell onto the track at the opening of the Manchester Liverpool Railway on 15 September 1830. He is commemorated in a fine monument in Chichester Cathedral, as he had been MP for the city before moving to Liverpool.

At noon on 4 August 1885, Magnus Volk opened the first electric railway to provide a regular service in Britain in his home town of Brighton, carrying the Mayor and other VIPs. He had obtained permission from the Corporation to

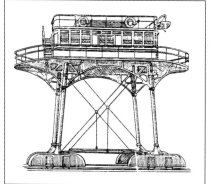 build a short line on the seafront and J T Chappell of Brighton laid a light 2ft gauge track on a shingle embankment. Another local engineer, Pollard of Church Street, built a simple four-wheeled car which was powered by Volk's 50 volt power plant.

The Bluebell Railway opened for business in 1960 as England's first standard gauge passenger-carrying preserved steam railway. British Rail had closed the Lewes to East Grinstead line, but the Bluebell Railway enthusiasts managed to acquire the freehold of the line and stations at Sheffield Park and Horsted Keynes. In 1975 the West

Hoathly station site was added and ten years later the Bluebell Railway acquired Kingscote Station, with permission to extend to East Grinstead.

The avalanche at Lewes on 27 December 1836 was the worst recorded in Britain. An eye-witness wrote: 'Between 10 and 11 in the Morning a great fall of Snow took place opposite Bolder Row (the parish houses) forced them down, and burrying in the Ruins fourteen persons, 8 of whom were taken out dead.' A memorial to those who died is on view in South Malling church and the name of the Snowdrop Inn in South Street is a reminder of the tragedy.

John Logie Baird made the first steps in his invention of television whilst recuperating at Hastings. The story can be seen at Hastings Museum. Baird wrote: 'When I arrived in Hastings in 1923 I came in search of health after a serious illness and thought I should never be fit and well again, but in a very short time the exhilarating atmosphere of Hastings made me a changed man. While down here doing nothing I took up the study of television again. I had been interested in it since my youth, and … with the aid of sound apparatus I managed to get together and the cordial assistance of a number of the Hastings residents … I soon began to get shadowy images to appear on the television screen.'

☆ ☆ ☆

When his Sussex novel became popular Graham Greene wrote to his brother Hugh, on 7 April 1939: 'A new shade for knickers and nightdresses has been named *Brighton Rock* by Peter Jones. Is this fame?'

☆ ☆ ☆

Anita Roddick opened her first shop in Kensington Gardens, Brighton in 1976 with a stock of fifteen products in plastic bottles with her own handwritten labels. This expanded to become Body Shop International plc, operating from her native town of Littlehampton, and its dynamic founder has been Businesswoman of the Year and Communicator of the Year.

Britain's oldest licensed airfield is at Shoreham. It was in a shed on what is now Shoreham Airport that Hal Piffard built the pusher biplane in which he made the first recorded flight from there on 10 July 1910.

On 20 June 1911 the new Brighton and Shoreham Aerodrome was opened by the mayors of Brighton, Hove and Worthing. Plans for the Terminal Building were drawn up by Stavers H Tiltman, resulting in an architectural triumph of art deco. The new Brighton, Hove and

Worthing Municipal Airport opened to the public on 13 June 1936 and thrives to this day.

Neville Duke flew from Tangmere in 1953 and broke the world air speed record at 727 mph in a Hawker Hunter jet fighter. There was an airfield here in the First World War and in the Second World War it was a Fighter Command station with links with Sir Douglas Bader, after whom the village pub is named. Hurricanes flew from here during the Battle of Britain and it was targeted by the Luftwaffe. In one raid German aircraft managed to destroy fourteen planes on the ground. Later Tangmere was used as a base for Lysanders and today it houses an aviation museum which is a reminder of its past.

Gatwick Airport was for some time the second busiest in the world, behind Heathrow, though it has now been overtaken. It had been licensed as a private airstrip in the 1930s but became London's second airport in 1974. From 1995 to 1999 it was voted the best UK airport and caters for more than 30 million passengers a year.

☆ ☆ ☆

The sunniest year in Sussex was 1949 when Eastbourne had a total of 2,153 hours of sunshine. Eastbourne vies with Jersey as the sunniest seaside resort in the British Isles.

☆ ☆ ☆

The heaviest hailstone ever recorded in Britain fell on Horsham on 5 September 1958. It weighed five ounces and was the size of a tennis ball.

In the hurricane of 16 October 1987 fifteen million trees were blown down, Petworth lost trees planted by Capability Brown in the 1750s including the largest sweet chestnut ever recorded.

Nymans at Handcross lost twenty eight trees which were champions, the tallest or largest in girth of their kind. Only eight survived. It also lost one of the largest Monkey Puzzle (Chile Pine) trees in the country.

Nymans a decade later, all its storm scars healed.

The Spirit of Sussex

The Old Town of Eastbourne in the Valley.
Watercolour by Louisa C Paris (1813-1875)

William Cobbett, writing of Lewes in 1822, found 'the girls remarkably pretty, as, indeed, they are in most parts of Sussex; round faces, features small, little hands and wrists, plump arms, and bright eyes. The Sussex men, too, are remarkable for their good looks.'

Sussex is certainly a happy place; and Felpham in particular is the sweetest spot on earth. Heaven opens here on all sides its golden gates. The windows are not obstructed by vapours. Voices of the celestial inhabitants are more distinctly heard, their form more distinctly seen; and my cottage is also a shadow of their houses.'

So wrote the poet William Blake who lived at Felpham near Bognor from 1800 to 1803.

Blake's cottage at Felpham.

In 1773 the great naturalist Gilbert White wrote: 'Though I have now travelled the Sussex downs upwards of thirty years, yet I still investigate that chain of majestic mountains with fresh admiration year by year, and I think see new beauties in it every time I traverse'.

The landscape from Newhaven to Lewes was a favourite with the poet, Coventry Patmore, who wrote in 1886: 'I do not know of a lovelier walk of eight miles. During the last half of the walk Lewes is always in sight; and if there is a setting sun upon it and the evening is calm, the views have a quality of quietness, peace, humility and pathos, which I have rarely seen elsewhere.'

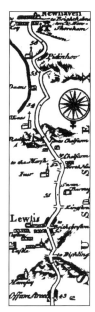

The Newhaven to Lewes section from **Britannia Depicta** *of 1751,*
'being a correct copy of Mr Ogilby's actual survey'.

View of Lewes 1787
An engraving by L. Middiman from a painting by C. Ostowell

In a guidebook of 1893 the South Downs were described as: 'the glory of Lewes. Covered with crisp turf, and dotted here and there with forests of heather, these magnificent hills seem to endow the pedestrian with health and hope at each step he takes, and carry the man back to boyhood days, away from all the cares and anxiety of life . . . The chief summits in the vicinity of the town are Mount Harry (639 feet), Mount Caburn (492 feet), Firle Beacon (718 feet), and Newmarket Hill (645 feet). From each of these magnificent views of a richly cultivated country may be obtained; and the visitor who would know how glorious a county Sussex is, must look upon it from a point of vantage. Nowhere in the County may such essentially English landscapes be found, as in no other part a town with such purely national characteristics as Lewes be found.'

Henry Hawkins, first chaplain of the Sussex Lunatic Asylum at Haywards Heath wrote in 1869: 'Here and there the spire and tower of a country church adds beauty to the scenery. Now and then the line of white vapour shows the course of a distant train. Further off are the softly undulating South Downs hills, presenting endless varieties of beauty. They delight the eye under almost every change of season and weather, sometimes appearing nearer to the eye – ominous, then, of bad weather – sometimes more remote; sometimes standing clear and bright in the sunshine, or overshadowed by the passing cloud, or partly shrouded by mist, or at times in winter capped or covered in snow.'

Esther Meynell claimed that: ' . . . the Downs of Central Sussex deserve praise in that they are most truly typical of all one means when one speaks of the South Downs. The simplicity of their line, hardly broken by anything bigger than a twisted thorn bush or a patch of gorse, is more significantly Sussex than Arundel's great woods sweeping across the curved hills. From the shoulder of Wolstonbury to the blunt nose of Firle Beacon looking across the gap to The Caburn, what a marvellous range it is, so bare, so beautiful, with its small incidents like Clayton windmills and the thin windswept clump of trees on Black Cap, gaining an almost fantastic value from the great simplicity of that line.'

In 1883 the American, John Burroughs, remarked: 'The South Downs form a very remarkable feature of this part of England, and are totally unlike any other landscape I ever saw. I believe it is Huxley who applies to them the epithet of muttony, which they certainly deserve, for they are like the backs of immense sheep, smooth, and round, and fat…'

In his autobiography Eric Gill reminisced: 'Lewes, to my mind, is a lovely town (though I've heard it called a 'dirty old place'), the playing field in the bottom under the Castle and the High Street climbing the hill – Shoreham with its splendid church and the harbour, Steyning and the Ouse River under the Downs, and Patcham and Poynings and Bramber and Beeding, Pyecombe and over the hill to Clayton and Ditchling – in those days, before motor-cars and motor-buses, these places were all unspoiled and untouched. And perhaps before and above and beyond all such things there were the Downs. If you have been a little child brought up in those hills and in those days, you will understand their mortal loveliness. If in your childhood, you have walked over them and in them and under them; if you have seen their sweeping roundness and the mists on them; and the sheep, and the little farmsteads in the bottoms, then you will know what I am talking about – but not otherwise. No one who was not there as a child can know that heaven, no grown-up can capture it.'

Leonard and Virginia Woolf settled at Asham below Itford Hill in 1912 and he wrote: 'This was the first time I had seen the South Downs as it were from the inside and felt the beauty of the gentle white curves of the hollows. I have lived close to them ever since and have learnt that, in all seasons and circumstances, their physical loveliness and serenity can make one's happiness exquisite and assuage one's misery.'

The Coombe, Lewes - showing 'the Downs flaring and scooped.'

Alan Rose in *Coastwise Lights* of 1990 wrote: 'Although I have spent more of my time in London, the emotional centre of my universe has always been Sussex; not Belloc's or Kipling's Sussex nor Bloomsbury's either, but somewhere between all of them, geographically as well as spiritually. The Sussex in my mind has white Saxon roads and Roman villas, squat downland churches with steep roofs and shingled spires that rise from encircling yews. The wall paintings, as at Clayton and Westmeston, will have been the work of Cluniac monks boarded at Lewes. It is a Sussex painted by William Nicholson and Eric Ravilious, the Downs flaring and scooped, sea in the air and in the light.

In *Iter Sussexiense*, which Dr John Burton wrote in 1751, he posed the question: 'Why is it that the oxen, the swine, the women, and all other animals, are so long-legged in Sussex?'

And this was his answer: 'May it be from the difficulty of pulling the feet out of so much mud by the strength of the ankle, that the muscles get stretched, as it were, and the bones lengthened?'

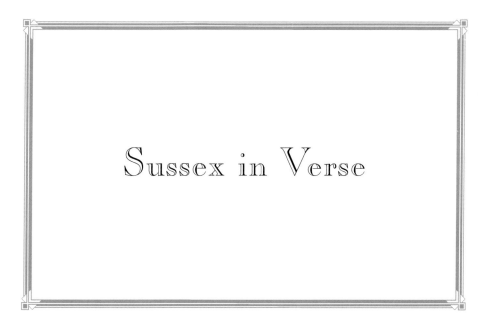

Sussex in Verse

From
SUSSEX BY THE SEA

(the chorus of which is still sung lustily on civic occasions and at formal dinners)

For we're the men from Sussex
Sussex by the sea,
We plough and sow and reap and mow,
And useful men are we:
And when you go from Sussex,
Whoever you may be,
You may tell them all that we stand or fall
For Sussex by the sea.

Oh Sussex, Sussex by the sea
Good old Sussex by the sea
You may tell them all that we stand or fall
For Sussex by the sea.

RUDYARD KIPLING

From
PROLOGUE TO GENERAL HAMLEY

Our birches yellowing, and from each
The light leaf falling fast
While squirrels from our fairy beech
Were bearing off the mast:
You came, and looked and loved the view,
Long-known and loved by me,
Green Sussex fading into blue
With one gray glimpse of sea.

*(Alfred, Lord Tennyson about his favourite Sussex vantage point at
Black Down on the North Downs, the highest point in Sussex. The Poet Laureate
had a house built at nearby Aldworth, laying the foundation stone on 23 April
1867. It was his last home, he died there in 1892)*

From
SUSSEX

I will go out against the sun
Where the rolled scarp retires,
And the Long Man of Wilmington
Looks naked towards the shires;
And east till doubling Rother crawls
To find the fickle tide,
By dry and sea-forgotten walls,
Our ports of stranded pride...

And here the sea-frogs lap and cling
And here, each warning each,
The sheep-bells and the ship-bells ring
Along the hidden beach

RUDYARD KIPLING

Shoreham - 'crowned with the grace of years'.

Rose-red eve on the seas that heave, sinks fair as dawn when the first ray peers;
Winds are glancing from sunbright Lancing to Shoreham, crowned with the grace of years;
Shoreham, clad with sunset, glad and grave with glory that death reveres.

From *On the South Coast* by ALGERNON CHARLES SWINBURNE.

As Sussex men that dwell upon the shore
Look out when storms arise and billows roar;
Devoutly praying with uplifted hands
That some well-laden ship may strike the sands;
To whose rich cargo they may make pretence
And fatten on the spoils of Providence,
So critics throng to see a new play split
And thrive and prosper on the wrecks of wit.

WILLIAM WYCHERLEY (1640-1716)

in *The Morning Bride*

From
THE SOUTH COUNTRY

When I am living in the Midlands
That are sodden and unkind,
I light my lamp in the evening,
My work is left behind;
And the great hills of the South Country
Come back into my mind.

The great hills of the South Country
They stand along the sea;
And it's there walking in the high woods
That I could wish to be,
And the men that were men when I was a boy
Walking along with me.

HILAIRE BELLOC

WEST SUSSEX DRINKING SONG

They sell good beer at Haslemere
And under Guildford Hill;
At little Cowfold, as I've been told,
A beggar may drink its fill.
There is a good brew in Amberley too,
And by the bridge also;
But the swipes they take in at Washington Inn
Is the very best Beer I know.

HILAIRE BELLOC

Away to sweet Felpham, for Heaven is there;
The Ladder of Angels descends through the air;
On the turret its spiral does softly descend,
Through the village then winds, at my cot it does end.

You stand in the village and look up to Heaven;
The precious stones glitter on flight seventy-seven;
And my brother is there, and the friends and thine
Descend and ascend with the bread and the wine.

The bread of sweet thoughts and the wine of delight
Feed the village of Felpham by day and by night,
And at his own door the bless'd hermit does stand
Dispensing unceasing to all the wide land.

WILLIAM BLAKE was in a mystic mood when he wrote these lines
about Felpham in a letter to a friend, Mrs Flaxman, in 1808.

Field Place, Broadbridge Heath, Horsham, the birthplace of Percy Bysshe Shelley (1792-1822)

THE SUSSEX MUSE

When Shelley's soul was carried through the air
Toward the manor house where he was born,
I danced along the avenue at Denne,
And praised the grace of Heaven, and the morn
Which numbered with the sons of Sussex men
A genius so rare!
So high an honour and so dear a birth,
That, though the Horsham folk may little care
To laud the favour of his birthplace there,
My name is bless'd for it throughout the earth.

C W DALMON

The Sussex Men are Noted Fools,
And weak is their brain-pan:
I wonder if H—   the painter
Is not a Sussex Man?

WILLIAM BLAKE *again, this
time in waspish mood.*

. . . .

If Bonyparte should have the heart
To land on Pens'ny Levels,
Then English sons with English guns
will blow him to the Devil.
(Traditional rhyme)

Sussex Buildings

and the Long Man

The Long Man of Wilmington has been called the largest representation in the world of the human form.

He is 235ft tall and has been variously identified as Pol or Balder, the old Saxon Sun God, pushing aside the doors of darkness; as the deity Varuna, worshipped in the Bronze Age and traditionally represented as opening the gates of Heaven; as the Celtic god Heil; the Nordic Wotan and many more mythical deities. His dates vary just as much – from Neolithic via Bronze Age to the eighteenth century classical revival period of folly building and antiquing the landscape.

The situation was summed up by a nineteenth century vicar of Wilmington – 'the Giant keeps his secret and from his hillside flings out a perpetual challenge'.

The 9th Duke of Devonshire conveyed the Long Man and two acres of land surrounding the figure to the Sussex Archaeological Trust in 1925. During the Second World War the white chalk outline of the giant had to be painted green to stop enemy aviators using it as a landmark.

The Pells in Lewes is one of the first public open-air swimming pools in England, opening in 1860, and paid for by public subscription.

The Church of St Nicholas at Worth is said to have 'the unique distinction of being the only Saxon cruciform edifice in the country that is complete and untouched in plan.' Despite a fire which destroyed the nave roof in 1986, it is a grand reminder of pre-Norman architecture.

Chichester is said to have the only cathedral spire in the country that is visible from the sea. It is also the only medieval cathedral in Great Britain to have a detached bell-tower.

Chichester Cathederal's 272ft high spire.

Bodiam Castle. Photo: *Sussex County Magazine*

Bodiam Castle has been described as 'the perfect model castle from the age of chivalry.' It was in 1385 that Sir Edward Dalyngrigge applied to Richard II for a Royal licence to fortify his manor house at Bodiam 'for the defence of the adjacent country' which at the time was under quite frequent attack from the French. He chose a new site in the Rother valley and his builder created a military fortification which was also a comfortable home complete with fireplaces and other domestic comforts. Bodiam was never attacked by the marauders against whom it had been built and surrendered with little or no siege to the forces of the Lancastrian Henry in the third War of the Roses. The castle was dismantled in the Civil War but was brought back to its full glory by Lord Curzon who acquired it in 1917. He bequeathed the site to the National Trust after his death in 1925.

Lullington is one claimant as the smallest church in England. It is now about 16 feet square and the remnant of the chancel of a thirteenth century church.

The extravagant eastern facade of the Royal Pavilion, Brighton, designed by John Nash for the Prince Regent from 1815.

William Hazlitt (1778-1830) described the Royal Pavilion at Brighton as being like a collection of stone pumpkins and pepperboxes. To his contemporary – essayist and wit, Sidney Smith – it appeared that 'the Dome of St Paul's had come down to Brighton and pupped'.

The marine pavilion was the centre of the social world during the season. On 29 October 1805 Mrs Creevey wrote to her husband about a party at 'this wicked Pavillion' in Brighton: 'The Prince led all the party to the table where the maps lie, to see him shoot with an air-gun at a target placed at the end of the room. He did it very skilfully, and wanted all the ladies to attempt it. The girls and I excused ourselves on account of our short sight; but Lady Downshire hit a fiddler in the dining-room, Miss Johnstone a door and Bloomfield the ceiling … I soon had enough of this, and retired to the fire with Mac.'

The half-timbered and thatched Old Clergy House at Alfriston was the first building to be bought by the National Trust. The Trust acquired it in 1896 for £10 from the Ecclesiastical Commissioners who, in 1885, had agreed to demolish this fourteenth century Wealden hall-house.

Arundel Cathedral was originally the Roman Catholic church of St Philip Neri. It was designed in 1868-9 and built in 1870-3 by J Aloysius Hansom, who was also the designer of the London Hansom cab. The church was built at the expense of the 15th Duke of Norfolk, to commemorate his coming of age.

The West Pier in Brighton is in the middle of a long-standing programme of conservation. It was designed and engineered by Eugenius Birch and opened in 1866. It is the only Grade I listed pier in England and closed to the public in 1975. the Brighton West Pier Trust was created to save the pier and return it to use.

Sussex and Nature

Hickstead was famous for Sussex spaniels, although the breed was becoming rare in 1871, giving way to pointers and setters. The Sussex spaniel is a dark liver colour, without any white about it, long ears, occasionally slightly curling, and the ends of which are of a lighter tint; it should be smooth and short-coated, long in the body, and low in the legs, with good broad feet, not flued in any part; the tail should have but little hair on it; the head should be long and broad across the forehead, and free from curls; and the whole expression of the animal should be lively and intelligent.

✳ ✳ ✳

Southdown sheep were brought to perfection by John Ellman of Glynde (1753-1832). Arthur Young wrote of them: 'The shoulders are wide; they are round and straight in the barrel; broad upon the loin and the hips; shut well in the twist, which is a projection of flesh in the inner part of the thigh that gives a fulness when viewed behind, and makes a South Down leg of mutton remarkably round and short, more so than in most other breeds.' They provided cheap meat and the wool was used for blanket-making or knitting.

Champion Southdown ewe. Kent County Show, 1929.

※ ※ ※

William Cobbett wrote that Sussex cattle seemed to be 'red, loose-limbed, and, they say, a great deal better than the Devonshire.' The Child family had been breeding Sussex cattle as early as 1760 but it was not until 1819 when one is recorded as winning first prize at the Bramber Stock Show.

Thomas Child's obituary notice in the *Sussex Express* of 1854 commented:

'The Michelham breed is both hardy and of a kindly disposition, and though its dispersion may be a subject of regret, it will no doubt be of public advantage. Michelham Priory [pictured above] has for nearly a century obtained a certain notoriety arising in great measure from the spirit with which the Child family devoted themselves to maintaining the superiority and purity of the herd.'

It was an old Sussex custom to ring the hogs before the festival of St Michael and All Angels and they were to remain so ringed until the following feast of St John the Baptist, under pain of forfeiting to the lord of the manor 'for every hog, for every week, 3s. 4d'.

A nineteenth century writer claimed that 'the First of March was notable in Sussex for its peculiar association with fleas. Everyone apparently agreed that on this particular date the creatures woke up and began hopping about, and that this was therefore the moment to get rid of them, but the suggested methods differed sharply.'

Pulix irritans - the flea.

Charlton

The Charlton, near Goodwood, was the first pack to hunt foxes in England and was world famous until it disappeared in the early years of the nineteenth century. The Duke of Monmouth, illegitimate son of Charles II, loved the hunting at Charlton so much that he declared: 'When I become King of England I will come and keep my court in Charlton.'

In January 1738 the 2nd Duke of Richmond, master of the Charlton, had a run of ten hours from East Dean to the Arun after a vixen and he was in at the death, one of only three of those who started to achieve this.

In sixteenth to eighteenth century Sussex sources there are several references to the use of perforated lucky stones suspended from the dewlap to protect cattle from hags and pixies and the conditions they were believed to inflict.

When the very last mouse-eared bat died in Sussex, it became the first species of mammal to become extinct in Britain since the wolf in 1740. It was Britain's largest species of bat with a wing span of 18 inches, but only one male remained and he disappeared in 1992.

Fred the goldfish, *carassius auratus*, was owned by A P Wilson of Worthing and when he died on 1 August 1980, at the age of forty-one, he was in the *Guinness Book of Records* as the oldest known fish.

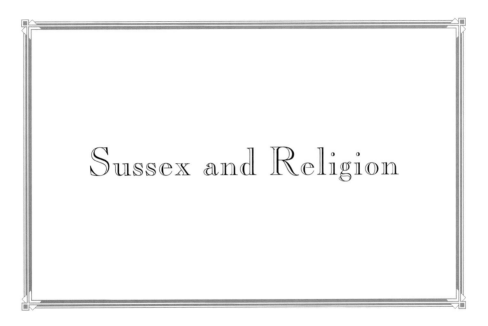

Sussex and Religion

Saint Wilfrid sailed to Sussex, an' he come to Selsey Bill,
An' there he built a liddle church upon a liddle hill:
He taught the starving pagans how to net fish from the sea,
An' then he them converted all to Christianitee.

SONG OF THE SUSSEX MEN *by Arthur Beckett, commemorating the conversion of Sussex in the 680s. It was the last county in England to become Christian.*

Saynt Dunstan (as the story goes)
Caught old Sathanus by the nose;
He tugged soe hard and made him roar,
That he was heard three miles and more.

This doggerel commemorates the occasion when the future Archbishop of Canterbury, while making a chalice in the forge at Mayfield, successfully routed the Devil, using hot tongs of Sussex iron. The devil appeared in female form to tempt Dunstan, who spotted his guest's cloven hoof and hurled him out so that he landed in Tunbridge Wells and plunged his sore nose into the local springs, giving them their chalybeate qualities.

The small towers, Battle Abbey.
Drawn on stone by G Rowe.

After winning the Battle of Hastings on 14 October 1066, William, Duke of Normandy vowed to build an abbey on the exact spot where God allowed him to conquer England.

The monks tried to build the abbey on more suitable land, further down the hill, but William insisted that it was built with the high altar over the spot where Harold fell. Battle Abbey was not consecrated until 1095 when William II, the Conqueror's son, presented to the abbey his father's gem-encrusted coronation robe and the sword he had used to ensure his victory.

✠ ✠ ✠

THANKS BE TO THEE my Lord Jesus Christ,
For all the benefits which Thou hast given me,
For all the pains and insults which Thou hast borne for me,
O most merciful Redeemer, Friend and Brother,
May I know Thee more clearly,
Love Thee more dearly
And follow Thee more nearly,
Amen.

*This is the prayer of St Richard, Bishop of Chichester from 1245
till his death in 1253 on 3 April which became his saint's day.
Part of this prayer was used centuries later in the musical* Godspell.

The Martyrs' Memorial

Richard Carver, a Brighton Quaker, was the mate on the *Surprise*, the vessel that carried Charles II to safety from Shoreham after his defeat at the Battle of Worcester in 1651. After the Restoration many of those involved with his escape to France asked the king for a reward, but Carver asked for the release from prison of some of his fellow Quakers and other persecuted non-conformists, including John Bunyan.

✠ ✠ ✠

Seventeen men and women were put to death for heresy in Lewes in the reign of Mary Tudor. The first to die bravely, on 22 June 1555, in the flames of the fire built outside the Star Inn was Derick Carver, a Flemish brewer who had made his home in Brighton. Lewes keeps their memory alive by the Martyrs' Memorial on Cliffe Hill and with the carrying of seventeen flaming crosses through the town on Bonfire Night.

✠ ✠ ✠

Daniel Defoe recorded: 'They have a story in this city [Chichester], that when ever a bishop of that diocese is to dye, a heron comes and sits upon the pinnacle of the spire of the cathedral: This accordingly happen'd, about – when Dr. – Williams was bishop: A butcher standing at his shop door, in the South-Street, saw it, and ran in for his gun, and being a good marks-man shot the heron, and kill'd it, at which his mother was very angry with him, and said he had kill'd the bishop, and the next day news came to the town that Dr. Williams, the last bishop was dead; this is affirm'd by many people inhabitants of this place'.

✠ ✠ ✠

*St Thomas's church, Winchelsea still
bears the scars inflicted by the French
in the fourteenth century*

Winchelsea was the site of the last of John Wesley's open-air sermons. Wesley recorded: 'I went over to that poor skeleton of ancient Winchelsea. I stood under a large tree and called to most of the inhabitants of the town, "The kingdom of heaven is at hand, repent and believe the gospel." It seemed as if all that heard were, for the present, almost persuaded to be christians.' The tree that he mentioned was blown down in 1927 but its scion, with a commemorative plaque, still flourishes in German Street.

✠　　✠　　✠

St Bartholomew's church in Brighton was built by Arthur Wagner, son of the Vicar of Brighton, to the exact biblical measurements of Noah's Ark. This meant that it measured 140 feet to the top of the cross, making it the tallest parish church in England.

Brighton Corporation was horrified by the height of the church and refused to grant permission for another building of the same proportions. Wagner got round this by excavating for the Church of the Resurrection so that one entered at the head of a mighty flight of steps.

St Bartholomew's church.

✠   ✠   ✠

Cardinal Manning, Archbishop of Westminster, started his career as an Anglican curate at Graffham. Towards the end of his career he admitted that time had not effaced everything. 'The past rises up to me … the Downs seem to me to be only less beautiful than Heaven … the little church under a green hillside where the morning and evening prayers, and the music of the English Bible, for seventeen years became part of my soul.'

✠　　✠　　✠

In October 1793 a clergyman in Lewes with a single discharge of his gun killed a partridge, shot a man, a hog, and a hogstye, broke fourteen panes of glass, and knocked down six gingerbread Kings and Queens that were standing on the mantelpiece opposite the window.

✠　　✠　　✠

Sussex Food and Drink

A VOLUPTUARY under the horrors of Digestion.

When Francis Grose toured Sussex in 1777, he noted in his Provincial Glossary: 'A Chichester lobster, a Selsey cockle, an Arundell mullett, a Pulborough eel, an Amberley trout, a Rye herring, a Bourne wheatear. These are all the best of their kind, at least of any that are taken in this county." In the mid nineteenth century these delightful birds visited the extensive downs between Eastbourne and Beachy Head from the end of July to the middle of September. One observer wrote: 'As they are then fat and of good flavour it is customary to dress them at the inns of the numerous watering places on the Sussex coast,' catching them in horsehair nooses set in tunnels under the turf.

Daniel Defoe toured England during 1724-26 and wrote of one Sussex town: 'This river, and the old decay'd, once famous castle at Arundel which are still belonging to the family of Howards, Earls of Arundel, a branch of the Norfolk family, is all that is remarkable here; except it be that in this river are catch'd the best mullets, and the largest in England, a fish very good in itself, and much valued by the gentry round, and often sent up to London.'

Grey mullet.

⏳ ⏳ ⏳

In her journal Celia Fiennes for 1697 recorded: "Rhye towne is not very bigg a little market place, this is famous for fish, from hence all the good Turbutt Pearle and Doria (= turbot, brill and John Dory) and all sort of sea fish comes to supply the Wells and London, but I could get little, the faire took up the fishermen; indeed here I drank right French white wine and exceeding good, and then returned to the Wells."

Richard Stapley of Hickstead Place wrote in his diary: 'In the month of November, 1692, there was a trout found in the Poyningeswish, in Twineham, which was 29 inches long from the top of the nose to the tip of the taile; and John fflint had him and eat him. He was left in a low slank after a ffloud, and the water fell away from him, and he died.'

Sussex Drip Pudding can be made according to the recipe of Mrs Eames of Manor Farm, Apuldram:

Make a suet pudding, and cook it the same day as the joint of beef. When meat is cooked, take it up, and then cut the suet pudding into slices and soak them each side in the dripping; put these on to a hot dish, and brown in the oven while making the gravy. Serve with the joint.

Most Sussex towns had markets. In 1804 Joseph Seagrave wrote of Chichester:

The weekly markets are held on Wednesdays and Saturdays; and are plentifully supplied from the country for several miles around, with various articles of daily consumption. During the season abundance of oysters are brought to the fish-shambles. . . the neighbouring coast supplies the market with plenty of lobsters, crabs, prawns, and several other kinds of fish – Worthing with makarel – and Arundel with mullet.

Chichester Market Cross

⧗ ⧗ ⧗

Sussex Pond Pudding was traditionally eaten on Palm Sunday in some places, whereas in others it was called Sussex Easter Pudding:

Make a good suet crust, put in some currants and a little sugar. Divide in two, and roll each piece into a rather thick round. Put into the middle of one round a ball of butter mixed with sugar, using the proportions of fi lb. Butter to fi lb. demerara sugar. Gather up the edges of the crust, and enclose the butter ball securely by covering the piece with the second round of crust. And pinching that up. Put in a floured cloth, tie up rather tightly, and boil them three hours or more according to size.

Bumboo was a Sussex drink made up of beer and brandy. Thomas Turner drank 'one bowl of punch and two mugs of bumboo' in 1756 at the Crown, the pub run by John Jones in East Hoathly.

'I spent 12d and came home in liquor! Oh! with what horrors does it fill my breast to think that I should be guilty of doing so – and on a Sunday, too.'

Esther Meynell noted: "There is a queer little legend attached to Chanctonbury that if anyone walks round the Ring on a moonless night seven times without stopping the Devil would come out of the wood and hand him a bowl of soup.

In 1797 'a bullock, which had been slaughtered for the purpose, was lately distributed, with a proportionate quantity of bread and coal, by order of John Cresset Pelham, Esq., one of the representatives in Parliament for Lewes, to such of his friends who chose to accept it. There were some who accepted the benevolence, who possessed the power of giving, instead of receiving, but it was pure election charity, and, therefore, all comment may be spared.' Afterwards bread and coals were distributed to more than 200 poor families in Lewes.

A horned sheep is basted by the official cook as it roasts over a fire built in Ebernoe fairground.

Photo: Sussex County Magazine

Ebernoe's Horn Fair has been celebrated for hundreds of years on or around 25 July, St James's Day. The *West Sussex Gazette* reported on the 1864 Horn Fair:

One of the most conspicuous objects of interest was the roasting of the horned sheep in the open air. A large group was gathered and notwithstanding the intense heat could not tear themselves away from the seething and sputtering object of their admiration.

The sheep horns go to the highest scorer in the cricket match played on the common that day between Ebernoe and a neighbouring village. The rest of the animal is eaten at so much a slice, with the proceeds going to charity.

An old Sussex riddle asked: 'Where is beer sold by the pound?' The answer is Bury, as the village beer house was next to the village pound.

The Reverend W D Parish in his 1875 *Dictionary of the Sussex Dialect* recorded:

A parishioner of mine once came to complain to me that her husband had threatened to ill-use her on account of two little pigs which rested on the fact that she was hobbing-up the pigs so carefully that she insisted on taking them to bed with her. I declined to interfere.

Sussex Sport and Leisure

Sussex County Cricket Club was founded in 1839, the first of the properly constituted county clubs. They played at first at a ground off Union Road, Brighton, called the Royal Ground thanks to the patronage of George IV. In 1847 they moved to the Brunswick Ground in Hove, still renowned as one of the truest pitches in England. Sussex won the first final of the Gillette Cup on 7 September 1963, beating Worcestershire by fourteen runs, thanks in part to their charismatic wicket-keeper, Jim Parks.

Willows grown in the Robertsbridge area have long been used to make cricket bats. These have been claimed to be the best in England and were used by the great W G Grace.

Following his tour of Australia with the England cricket team in 1891/2, the 3rd Earl of Sheffield donated £150 in appreciation of the hospitality extended to his party. The Australian Cricket Council used this money to provide a shield in 1892/3 for the competition between the Australian states which lasted for 100 years. The silver shield had an image of the Sheffield Park Cricket Ground as the centrepiece, as Australian teams used to begin their tours of England on this ground, long before Arundel Park had this distinction.

Sussex's only professional football club is Brighton and Hove Albion, which was founded in June 1901. They moved to the Goldstone Ground in Hove in 1902 but in recent times, after increasingly acrimonious public debate, they have left this base which has now been developed. The team plays at Withdean until a new stadium can be purpose-built. Their greatest day came in 1983 when they reached the F A Cup Final.

Sphairistike is the name of the game being played on an hour glass shaped court in Eastbourne's Devonshire Park. It was patented by Major Walter Wingfield in 1873 but the rules were so confusing – there was no limit to the number of serves each player could make, no allowance for double faults – that the Marylebone Cricket Club was asked to give some guidelines. These were not much help and it was not until the All England Croquet and Lawn Tennis Club set up its own committee in 1877 that matters were sorted out.

It was in 1874 that William Cavendish, 7th Duke of Devonshire, appropriated Devonshire Park 'for the purposes of cricket and as a recreation ground.' Today it has a £4.5million International Lawn Tennis Centre where, in the year 2000, the Eastbourne pre-Wimbledon ladies tennis tournament celebrated its twenty-fifth anniversary.

It is because of its grass courts, now with the turf from Wimbledon's old Court No 1 on its own No 1 court, that it attracts so many of the top players. They are anxious to practise on the unfamiliar surface before going on to compete in the only Grand Slam tournament still played on grass.

The British Marbles Championships are held at the Greyhound Inn in Tinsley Green, West Sussex. Up to 20 six-man teams assemble round a 6ft sand-filled ring in which forty-nine red marbles lie. They flick their own marbles from the edge of the ring, to knock the red marbles out. The first team to dispose of twenty-five marbles wins. It is said to date back to 1600 when two local men, from either side of the Surrey and Sussex border, competed for the affections of a beautiful village girl and decided who won her by playing a game of marbles.

⚑　　⚑　　⚑

The chess world's longest running annual tournament is the Hastings Congress held at the White Rock Pavilion. It attained its seventy-fifth year in 1999.

⚑　　⚑　　⚑

The Chichester Festival Theatre with its revolutionary in-the-round auditorium, opened in 1962 under the direction of Laurence Olivier. Major productions continue in the main building in the festival season, and now there is the smaller Minerva next door for more experimental work.

      🏴   🏴   🏴

The De La Warr Pavilion at Bexhill was the first public building in the country to have a welded steel frame. It was built in the 1930s by those two apostles of the functional style of architecture, Eric Mendelsohn and Serge Chermayeff. As did many other entertainment centres along the Sussex coast it offered repertory in spring, autumn and winter, a lavish pantomime at Christmas and a resident variety show for the summer season.

An hour long interval gives opera lovers a chance to eat al fresco in the gardens at Glyndebourne.

The great Welsh baritone, Sir Geraint Evans, said of Glyndebourne's founder, Sir George Christie's father:

As for John Christie, he was one of the great English eccentrics. How could he be otherwise when he built an opera house in the Sussex downs, fifty miles from London, assembled the finest international talent to perform in it, and expected the public not only to respond at higher than metropolitan ticket prices, but to put on evening dress in the middle of the afternoon to do so?

Yet he made Glyndebourne a name respected throughout the operatic world and laid the foundation of an opera festival in Britain which has greatly helped the development of the art and its wider enjoyment.

Sir George Christie declared: '1934 was the last time an opera house was specially built in this country. 1994 will see the next one. Both happen to be at Glyndebourne.'

Commercial film making started in Sussex in 1896 with the work of Robert William Paul. Many more followed but the only film studio complex was on Shoreham Beach from 1919 to 1923. In 1914 Francis Leonard Lyndhurst had formed the Sunny South Film Company and often used Shoreham Fort as a film set. Other companies succeeded this early one until film-making came to an end there when fire destroyed most of the studio buildings.

⚑ ⚑ ⚑

The Sussex Symphony Orchestra was formed in 1993, using players only from the county. In 1999 it produced its first CD of music composed and played by Sussex people.

⚑ ⚑ ⚑

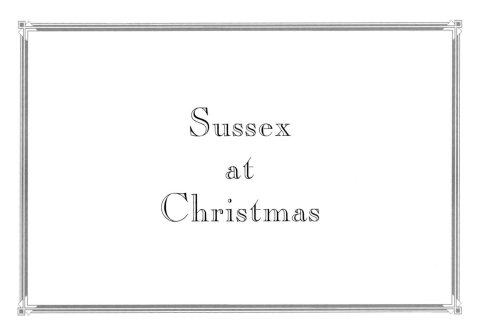

Sussex
at
Christmas

Observing the true traditions of Christmas, as practised in Sussex in days gone by, required an exceptional amount of energy and effort. Preparations began on Stir Up Sunday, the twenty-fifth after Trinity, so called because the collect for the day is:

Stir up, we beseech thee, O Lord, the wills of thy faithful people: that they, plenteously bringing forth the fruit of good works, may of thee be plenteously rewarded.

When the fruits and the fats, the nuts and the spices for the puddings and pies were partially blended everyone had a stir in order of seniority – first mother, then father followed by children in age order and other members of the household. And it was woe betide anyone who stirred widdershins. It was essential to stir sunwise, with a wooden spoon – and silently, with the eyes shut, make a secret wish. . .

❋ ❋ ❋

The poor of the parish had to beg their way to a part in the Christmas plenty. On Gooding Day, 21 December, according to Sussex historian Mark

Antony Lower, writing in 1861: '. . . the old women of every parish went from house to house to beg something to provide for the festivities of Christmas. The miller gave each dame a little flour, the grocer a few raisins, the butcher an odd bit of beef, and so on. From persons not in trade a donation in money was expected.'

❋ ❋ ❋

'I never saw a Christmas tree before, and enjoyed it like a child. It was far prettier than I expected. Four fir trees, two very large and two small, in big pots covered with gold apples and silver pears and every kind of pink, blue and green cornucopias filled with bon-bons.' So wrote Lucy Hare, to her sister, after she had seen the first Christmas tree in Sussex at Herstmonceux Place in 1843.

There were many local carols – from Ringmer, Ditchling, Burwash – but the most famous is the Sussex Carol

On Christmas Night all Christians Sing
To hear the news the angels bring.
News of great joy, news of great mirth
News of our Saviour king's birth.

This was given to Ralph Vaughan Williams by Mrs Verrall of Monks Gate and formed a long-lasting part of his desire to 'make his art an expression of the whole life of the community'.

Christmas was not always celebrated with a turkey. Thomas Turner, who lived at East Hoathly, spent 25 December 1756 'at home all day. No churching here the whole day. James Marchant and the widow Caine dined with us on a sirloin of beef roasted in the oven with a batter pudding under it, a plum suet pudding, boiled potatoes and some bullace pies. In the even Tho. Davy sat with us about 3 hours and to whom and in the day I read 7 of Tillotson's sermons.'

This menu occurs, with minor variations, for every Christmas mentioned in his diary.

Mrs Henry Dudeney in Lewes described her celebration on 25 December 1928:

Christmas Day. Communion at 7.45, then breakfast, presents: I gave Ernest a walking stick and he gave me a bag. More church! A little dim walk in the afternoon by the river, just me and Emma. Basement rooms and front parlours all lighted up and curtains drawn. Doleful sounds of festivity – mouth organs or gramophones – stealing out into the mist.

In 1933 Virginia Woolf wrote to her nephew, Quentin Bell: This is a black foggy Christmas week; and the human race is distracted and unlovable.

That is, I spent yesterday in Oxford Street buying things like gloves and stockings. A drought is imminent; Rodmell has long since ceased to wash; and it is said that Communion is no longer possible, owing to the congealed state of the holy blood. We go down today and I shall think of you when the owl comes out of the ivy bush and the bells.'

It's six o'clock on a Christmas morn.
Mistresses arise and let your maids lie still
For they have risen all the year,
Much against their will.
(*Lewes town cry*)

On New Year's Eve was the Apple Howling, when the parish youths visited the various orchards and whacked the apple trees so that they should bear a good crop the following year.

New Year's Day was not always kept as a holiday. On Sunday 1 January 1758 Thomas Turner recorded in his diary:

I gave my cousin John Bennett 12d. in order for him to buy for me at Edm. Baker's circulating library Budgen's account of the hurricane in Sussex in 1729.

INDEX